The *Student Essentials* series

STUDENT
ESSENTIALS

Dissertation

Jessica Cooper

trotman | t

Student Essentials: Dissertation

This first edition published in 2011 by Trotman Publishing, a division of Crimson Publishing Ltd, Westminster House, Kew Road, Richmond, Surrey TW9 2ND

© Trotman Publishing 2011

Author Jessica Cooper

Designed by Andy Prior

British Library Cataloguing in Publication Data
A catalogue record for this book is available from the British Library

ISBN 978 1 84455 420 1

Typeset by IDSUK (DataConnection) Ltd

Printed and bound in the UK by Ashford Colour Press, Gosport, Hants

Contents

Introduction

The dissertation is a 'longitudinal project' which takes months, and in some cases a year or more, to complete. It is a style of assessment which you may not have encountered before, so this could mean learning a lot of new skills in a short space of time. You may be excited by this prospect, or possibly a little scared, but as long as you know what is expected of you, the dissertation should not pose you any major problems.

The exciting thing about the dissertation is that you have the opportunity to take full ownership of your project. This means that you are responsible for everything, from finding out what to study, to finding out how to study it.

Unlike an essay, the dissertation is not a linear process and it doesn't follow a neat chronological order, although it must be presented as such in the final written paper. Simply put, you start the dissertation process in the middle (choosing your topic, doing background reading and designing a research proposal), move to the end (the results and conclusion) and end at the start (the introduction). Sometimes you need to go back and reinterpret or re-evaluate a claim as a result of new findings. You may find that you go back to the same point in the process several times. This isn't as laborious as it sounds. Each time you go back you will have more knowledge – and having more knowledge means being able to see the situation in a different way than before.

Before you begin your dissertation there are a few things that you should find out. These can influence the initial decisions you make and should be your first priority.

- Find out how long the dissertation will be – ask your department for a handbook of guidelines.
- Find out the submission date (it seems obvious, but it's easy to get caught out!).
- Find out if there are any official deadlines between starting and finishing – perhaps you have to hand in a proposal, or a copy of your research proposal.
- Find out how you are expected to carry out your research – there may be rules you must follow.
- Find out what the assessment criteria are – they may be different from the criteria used to mark exams and coursework.
- Find out how many chapters there should be and whether you need to include an abstract (a short summary of the work).
- Find out how your department wants the dissertation to look – they may expect it to be bound.

There are two final things to think about before you set off on your dissertation journey.

1. You are writing the dissertation to obtain credits which will help you achieve a degree classification you are happy with. Keep this in the back of your mind throughout the dissertation process.

2. Don't do anything rash or risky – a dissertation is not the place to test established practices of assessment. Using humour or methods which are out of the ordinary won't win you rewards.

NB: the terms 'dissertation', 'research project' and 'independent enquiry' are all used interchangeably in this guide. There is also a glossary at the end of the book in case you need guidance on any of the terms that are used. It can be a minefield!

PART 1

Preparing for your dissertation

Writing a dissertation means having to think on your feet and adjust to a new type of assessment while you are doing it! To help you face this challenge head on, Chapters 1 and 2 of this study guide show you how to organise your time, plan your project and narrow down your area of focus. Chapter 3 tells you about the two main types of research and which disciplines they are most suitable for.

1 Preparing and planning

Writing your dissertation is possibly the biggest task you will have to undertake as an undergraduate. You may feel daunted, but remember that this is a fantastic opportunity for you to show yourself and your lecturers how much your academic skills have developed over the course of your studies.

The differences between an essay and a dissertation

The dissertation is different from undergraduate essays you have previously written. To get top marks you have to show that you are able to make the adjustment from essay to larger research project. This means understanding the differences between the two different types of writing.

So, what are the main differences?

Essay	Dissertation
No chapters	Between five and nine chapters (this depends on the faculty you are in)
Your tutor gives you the topic to research (although in some cases you may be able to choose your title)	In most subject areas you are completely free to choose your area of study
2,500 word count limit (or less)	5,000–10,000 word count limit

Requires secondary research	Requires primary research and in-depth analysis of secondary sources (see Chapter 3)
Takes a few weeks to research and write	Takes four months to a year to plan, research and write
Needs to answer the question	Needs to be original (something that you do by yourself, for yourself)

Identifying the different stages

Having an idea of how the different pieces all fit together gives you a clear overview of the dissertation. It also helps you to stay focused on the end result.

We will look at each of the stages in more detail later in the book, but here is a brief overview of the different tasks involved in writing a dissertation:

- choosing a topic (see Chapter 2)
- background reading (see Chapter 2)
- narrowing down your focus (see Chapter 2)
- choosing a question or hypothesis (see Chapter 2)
- designing a research proposal (see Chapters 3 and 4)
- reviewing the literature (see Chapter 5)
- planning your methods of data collection (see Chapter 4)
- analysing your sources (see Chapter 6)
- describing your findings (see Chapter 6)
- drawing logical conclusions (see Chapter 7)
- constructing a logical argument (see Chapter 7)
- making an outline (see Chapter 8)
- referencing your sources (see Chapter 9)
- writing your introduction (see Chapter 8)
- proofreading (see Chapter 9).

Setting and managing deadlines

It is helpful to have targets and deadlines in your dissertation as it breaks the work down into manageable chunks. Manageable chunks are easier to monitor than large chunks and enable you to assess the progress you are making. Small chunks also stop you feeling overwhelmed by the enormity of the task.

Although the dissertation process is not a chronological one, having a linear overview of the tasks as well as a timetable will help you keep track of your project.

Before you draw up a timetable you will need to find out the following:

QUICK TIP

If you draw up a timetable, remember that many of the tasks will be happening simultaneously.

- the official date when you are expected to begin 'engaging' with the dissertation (check your department guidelines)
- the submission deadline (starting four months before the deadline is just about adequate to pass the dissertation, though unrealistic if you want to get a first. Some colleges and universities advise you to begin preparation in the year prior to submission)
- roughly how long each stage will take (ask your supervisor).

Try to be realistic when setting deadlines – failing to meet a deadline can throw the whole project out of sync. Bear in mind that your supervisor may have external commitments, such as a research sabbatical, which can hold up work on the dissertation. Remember to build these into your schedule.

What to do if you miss one of your deadlines

Failing to meet an unofficial or informal deadline isn't the end of the world. However, it might suggest you are taking too much time on tasks, or that you set unrealistic timeframes in the beginning. Go back through the project and have another look at the deadlines you have set. Think about the following questions.

- Are you trying to do too much in too short a space of time? Go back to your research aim (see Chapter 2) and re-evaluate whether what you are proposing is possible.
- Are you including too much detail? Check the assessment criteria to see if this level of detail is needed.
- Are you taking too long because you're finding this section difficult? Consider putting that particular section to one side and coming back to it at a later stage.
- Are you waiting for other people? Can you progress without their responses or feedback?

Know your style of working

People approach their work in different ways and the dissertation is no exception. Try to find a way to use your own approach to your advantage. To do this think about the way you approach essay writing. Ask yourself the following questions.

Do you tend to leave everything to the last minute?

This approach doesn't work well with research, especially if you need to generate your own data. Having data ready well in advance is especially helpful if there are unforeseen problems; for instance, you don't manage to generate the statistics you need and have to start all over again.

Do you work better in the morning or do you prefer to work late at night?

If you prefer to work at night, make sure that you schedule your work sessions for this time. But remember: just because you work at night doesn't mean that everyone else does. You might have to work during the day as well, especially if you have to collect data.

Do you struggle to meet word counts?

Ask yourself if you have enough 'content' to work with. Difficulty to reach a word count could reflect a lack of input. Make sure you have read a sufficient amount and that you have generated enough data. Alternatively, too many words can mean that you have not been concise enough. Go back through your work and check that all your text is relevant to the chapter, and to your aims and objectives.

Working with your supervisor

Your supervisor is one of the people responsible for marking your dissertation. They generally know a lot about the field in which you are writing and often are a lecturer with whom you have already worked.

A good supervisor is supportive and objective and will highlight the things you are doing well, as well as the things you need to improve. It is their job to offer you constructive advice and ask questions to guide your thinking. They will try to raise your awareness of the areas in which you need to think more critically and the areas in which you need to be more focused. You will be expected to meet

> **QUICK TIP**
>
> Remember: your supervisor is there to help you.

your supervisor at least once over the course of your dissertation but hopefully you will meet much more often than this.

The meetings

Arrange your first meeting in week one or two of your dissertation timetable. Use this meeting to discuss your ideas and your aims for the project. Make sure that you have something to discuss – even if you haven't yet come to a decision about your topic, ask some general questions. Here are some examples of questions you could ask.

- How many hours of self-study am I expected to put into this project?
- Which skills are you expecting me to display evidence of?
- Can I have a copy of the assessment criteria?

Before you leave your first meeting, make sure you organise a timetable of future meetings – your supervisor may not offer their time or help, they may wait for you to ask.

Use any other subsequent meetings to receive feedback on your research. Don't be afraid to discuss problems – it is the way in which you handle the problem that is important, not the fact that you had the problem in the first place.

QUICK TIP

Remember to keep a written record of what is said in this and all subsequent meetings. Try to do this as soon after the meeting as possible so you don't forget anything.

Supervisor problems

If you feel that your supervisor is not giving you the support you need, or that they are being overly critical, there are several options you can explore. The first is to accept that you have a difficult relationship – negative input can be constructive. If this seems impossible, option two is to speak to the course convenor about getting a different tutor assigned to your project. However, your supervisor may have specialist knowledge in the field you are studying and could be the best person for the job. Option three is to turn to your fellow students. Organise a study group – discuss your ideas, setbacks, successes and progress.

Tips for top scores

■ Write a short research proposal, even if this is not required. Take it with you to your first meeting with your supervisor. This will not only reflect well on your organisational skills, vision and focus, but will help you to articulate your ideas efficiently in your first meeting. You will be able to transform this proposal into your introduction (see Chapter 8) and methodology (see Chapter 4) in the writing-up process.

■ Familiarise yourself with the assessment criteria – these will be in your student handbook or available in the department. Don't be afraid to ask for clarification of what each of the criteria means. Not only will this make expectations clearer in your own mind, it will show that you are taking an active role in your own development.

■ When drawing up your timetable, factor in a few weeks of extra time for unforeseen circumstances. Things often go wrong or have a habit of taking longer than you imagined they would.

✓ Dos	✗ Don'ts
✓ Know the differences between an essay and a dissertation.	✗ Feel overwhelmed by the dissertation. It can be an enjoyable experience.
✓ Know when you officially have to start work on the dissertation.	✗ Leave everything until the last minute.
✓ Leave enough time for planning, researching, collecting data and writing.	✗ Make a plan and then never look at it again. Put it somewhere you will see it.
✓ Be realistic when setting your deadlines and planning anything related to the project.	✗ Worry if you miss a deadline. Just get back on track as soon as you can.
✓ Draw up a timetable of meetings with your supervisor.	✗ Wait for your supervisor to ask you questions – arrive at each meeting prepared and ready to take the initiative.

2 Choosing your topic

Many students find selecting a suitable and workable topic one of the most difficult processes in the dissertation project. Yet choosing the right topic is essential for your own motivation and for the viability of the project as a whole.

Defining and designing an independent enquiry is not an easy task and it is perfectly normal to feel a sense of rising panic at the very thought of it. But if you want your project to be successful you have to transform this panic into action.

For many undergraduates the dissertation is the first time you are in complete control of a project from the initial idea to the final word. But don't forget that you have been working towards this and building up the necessary skill set since you arrived at university, so you have absolutely nothing to be worried about!

Department restrictions on topic choice

Before you begin dreaming up your project, familiarise yourself with any restrictions your department may have on your choice of topic. Science students may find that they are working on projects which stem from the research interests of their tutors, whereas social science and humanities students may find no restrictions at all – a daunting prospect in itself.

Finding a topic that interests you

Your dissertation lasts for several months, so it is a good idea to choose a research topic that interests you. Try to find a topic for which you have intrinsic motivation – motivation to learn more about the topic for no other reason than learning itself. If you can match this with external motivation – motivation which brings rewards, such as a scholarship for a master's degree or career progression – then you will find the process of research far easier than if you are forcing yourself to investigate something you have little interest in.

So, how do you begin to find a topic? Think back over the modules you have studied and try to remember if something you read or learnt caught your eye. Did you touch upon an area of research in a seminar which you were unable to explore further because of time constraints? Did you score particularly highly on one module? Is this where your strengths lie?

Suggestions for topic inspiration

If you are still stuck for ideas, reflect on your own personal interests and hobbies. If you play a sport or take part in martial arts that originated in another country, could you investigate the origins of the sport, or think about how and why it has been accepted into UK society? If you are interested in cooking, is there a particular aspect or style of cuisine that you find interesting? Do you have a part-time job or did you work prior to coming to university? Could this work experience be made into a workable topic?

If you are still lost for ideas, ask the course convenor if you can view previous dissertations. This may give you an indication of the types of topic students have researched previously and generate inspiration. In some universities, past dissertations are readily available in the library.

Background reading

Background reading is essential when choosing a topic as it helps you to set your topic in context and informs you if the topic is workable. You may need to do background reading on several topics before you settle on one that you are happy with.

You don't need to read everything there is on the topic at this stage, but you should read extensively to inform yourself about the current debates and arguments and gaps in previous research and literature. You can talk about these with your supervisor in your first meeting.

Don't feel that you need to limit your background reading to academic texts alone at this stage. If you think reading journalistic pieces and web articles will advance your understanding of the topic, read these too (but be aware that these sources cannot be cited or used on your reference list as they are not 'academic').

We will go into more detail about reading in Chapter 5.

Narrowing down your focus

Once you have chosen a topic you should try to find a specific niche within it that you want to investigate. Identifying this niche isn't always easy – it requires critical thinking skills and a realistic assessment of what you will be able to achieve within the time available. Try not to be overambitious. Consult your dissertation guidelines, work out how much time you have, evaluate available resources, and decide what is achievable within those constraints.

QUICK TIP

Seek out the help, support and guidance of your supervisor if you feel a little lost at this stage. Don't be disconcerted or embarrassed by this – it is what they are there for. Your supervisor has considerably more experience of research than you do and can help you to focus your thoughts and settle on a topic.

Narrowing down a topic does not have to be difficult. By questioning your own ideas and identifying the different concepts and variables, you can narrow down the broadest topic area in no time at all.

Let's look at an example of narrowing down a large topic: a student has chosen to investigate *attitudes towards the rise in tuition fees*, but the subject is too broad for a 5,000–10,000-word undergraduate dissertation. The student needs to identify the different concepts within the topic and ask themselves a series of questions about each one in order to make the topic more focused. In this case, the different elements of the topic are:

- attitudes
- the rise
- tuition fees.

Here are some example questions the student could ask.

- Whose attitudes am I really interested in?
- Am I interested in investigating whether age influences attitudes?

- Am I interested in investigating whether social class influences attitudes? If so, how would I define 'social class' and how could I determine which social class someone belonged to?
- When I say 'attitudes', what exactly do I mean?
- Do I have an idea of what attitudes towards fees were before it was announced that they would be increased? How can I measure the change, if there is one?
- What do I know or what can I find out about the rise? How much have fees risen? Why have they risen? Does this rise have an effect on anything else? What do people feel about the effect?
- What are tuition fees? Who has to pay them? Where does the money come from?

Focusing and narrowing a topic requires eliminating potential areas for study. Bear in mind that sub-topics are always bigger than you originally imagine and in-depth knowledge is favourable to a superficial understanding of a topic. At the same time, don't eliminate all of your ideas until you have thought them through sufficiently and have decided that they are not tenable for a long-term project.

Going back to the example, let's imagine that the student is interested only in the attitudes of British students. The student wants to know if gender has an influence on attitude. By eliminating some of the ideas raised by questioning, the student is able to narrow down the focus of their topic to the following.

> " *The influence gender has on British students' attitudes towards the proposed rise in tuition fees.* "

NB: this is not a research question or even the title of a paper. It is only the specific area of the topic to be studied.

Types of dissertation

Now that you have a more focused research area, you can choose your dissertation type. There are three common categories:

1. asking a question and trying to answer it

2. identifying a problem and trying to find a solution to it

3. exploring a topic and trying to advance current knowledge and understanding.

Types one and two are easier for the novice researcher – they are more concrete in their objectives and outcomes. Type three can pose problems for a student who is unfamiliar with the research process. For the purposes of this study guide, we will be concentrating on types one and two only. If you are keen to proceed with type three and have a good, workable idea, talk it through with your supervisor before you commit any time or energy to the project.

Finding research questions and problems

Your dissertation will have either a research question or a hypothesis at the centre. A research question tries to find out new information, but a hypothesis sets out to prove whether something is true or false. They both need to be extremely focused.

Here is a list of things you should keep in mind when searching for your question or hypothesis.

- It should fulfil the department's assessment criteria.
- It should not be answerable or solvable with a one-word answer.
- It should not leave the reader thinking: 'And . . . so what?'

Identifying variables

Formulating research questions involves identifying a research problem, then working out which questions you need to ask to solve the problem. Identifying the variables (the elements that can be measured) in the topic can help you form the question. This means thinking about how many independent factors there are.

Let's take an example: imagine you are a strong advocate of organic food and you believe that organic food is better for health than non-organic. You want to ask the question: *Do people agree that organic food is better for health?* Asking a question like this could create misleading results: people may agree that it is better, but they may not actually eat organic food (because they think it is too expensive). This question is also insufficient as it can be answered by either 'yes' or 'no'. To make it more 'researchable', we could add variables, for example the influence of education on people's perceptions, or the proximity of where people live to available organic produce. Both of these factors can be measured. Other variable elements we could introduce are gender or age.

> **QUICK TIP**
> Although there will be a huge range of variables, refine your question to just two or three. This will keep you focused.

Formulating a hypothesis

This involves making a logical guess at what you think the outcome of the research will be, which means you need to know about the background to the problem you are hypothesising about. A hypothesis should be quite limited in the number of concepts and variables it contains, and, above all else, it should be testable.

Let's go back to the example about organic food. Based on what you know, you may choose to start with the hypothesis: *Women between the ages of 25 and 40 are more likely to buy organic food than men.* You could 'test' this hypothesis by disproving a null hypothesis (the opposite of what you really think) – in this case: *Women between the ages of 25 and 40 are less likely to buy organic food than men.*

Aims and objectives

Once you have a research question or hypothesis, begin setting out your aims and objectives. Your aim is the overall target of what you want to achieve in your research, and the objectives are the stepping stones you use to reach your aim. Once these are clear, transform them into a research proposal.

Tips for top scores

■ Make sure there is a good rationale for choosing your topic. Discuss it with your supervisor and don't just choose it because you think it is easy.

■ Once you have narrowed down your topic, explain it (in a couple of sentences) to someone who knows nothing about it. If they understand, you know your aim is clear and your research is focused.

✓ Dos	✗ Don'ts
✓ Find out about the limitations of topic choice in your department.	✗ Leave your topic choice to the last minute.
✓ Choose a topic that interests you.	✗ Choose a topic because you think it is easy.
✓ Read extensively about the topic.	✗ Ignore literature – background reading is essential.
✓ Ask yourself lots of questions about the topic.	✗ Choose a question that can be answered with a yes/no answer.
✓ Refine your question to include two or three variables.	✗ Choose a topic which has no scope for discussion.

3 Research

Before you get stuck into your dissertation, it is useful to learn about different types of research. This will help you to turn your ideas into practice and use the right approach.

Qualitative and quantitative research

Research can be broken down into two main approaches: qualitative and quantitative.

- Qualitative research is concerned with meaning and understanding.
- Quantitative research is concerned with quantity and accuracy.

Different academic disciplines tend to use different approaches. For example, the natural sciences, mathematics and engineering use quantitative research, whereas the social sciences, arts and humanities tend to use qualitative data. This is not a hard and fast distinction, so don't feel constrained to using one type only. If you have a genuine case for using qualitative data in a science dissertation and can explain your rationale, there is no reason why you shouldn't do this.

The boundaries between which approach different disciplines use are becoming increasingly blurred, but some departments still have strict regulations about which type of method they expect you to use. Make sure you know what is expected of you. If your department does not have any regulations, there are still expectations to meet – your supervisor will make a judgement about your choice of approach and an unwise choice could cost you marks. Speak to your supervisor if you're not sure.

Quantitative research

Quantitative research is an approach which is traditionally employed by, but not limited to, scientists, mathematicians, engineers, doctors and dentists. It typically involves identifying a concept and learning more about it. This is achieved through experiment, questionnaire and observation (see Chapter 4 for more on all of these). The quantitative approach focuses on accuracy and numbers and often has a hypothesis at the centre. It believes that the researcher is able to make logical, informed conclusions about knowledge that has been predetermined. This is often referred to as the 'positivist' approach.

Experiments enable a researcher to manipulate a single concept which may (or may not) influence the behaviour of another singular concept. By conducting experiments, researchers are able to collect data on the frequency and pattern of the behaviour. Experiments can be replicated time and time again because they are 'controlled'. This is helpful if you encounter a problem with your data and need to start all over again, or if you want to reproduce someone else's research.

This type of research is thought to be objective as opposed to subjective, meaning that the observer doesn't influence the collection of data directly.

Qualitative research

The qualitative approach, primarily used by researchers in the social sciences, arts and humanities, is different. It is concerned with beliefs and feelings. To generalise, it has words rather than numbers at its core. Qualitative researchers tend to begin with an observation and end with a hypothesis; this contrasts with the quantitative approach, where researchers begin with a hypothesis which is proved through observation.

Qualitative research is subjective and has feelings and behaviour as the basis of the research. It allows a researcher to categorise immeasurable data and make observations about broader social phenomena, such as identity, political ideologies or religion. An example of qualitative research would be an interview with international students to ascertain whether they believe they are getting value for money in their UK degree courses, or an exploration of all the critiques made about one particular author or film maker. This type of research believes that knowledge is constructed through interaction and that we arrive at knowledge through understanding.

Mixed approach

Research is not as black and white as it seems, especially when it comes to choosing an approach. You may find that you need to use a mixture of approaches. Let's look at a couple of examples where a mixed approach would be beneficial.

Example 1
A student of medicine conducts a survey to investigate whether a sample group take painkillers on a regular basis. He follows this up by finding out more about the group's belief systems towards the painkillers through interviews and/or a focus group.

Example 2

A humanities student wants to answer the question: 'What importance does race have in British identity?' He conducts interviews with several people and evaluates several forms of media, e.g. magazines and radio broadcasts. He then compares his results with established quantitative demographic data.

Using two different approaches together can add depth to the research, making it more reliable and more informative. However, using mixed methods means more organisation and thought on the part of the researcher. It can also be time consuming. Before using a mixed approach, you should think about questions such as: *'What will I do if the results from the two different methods don't match?'*

QUICK TIP

Remember: the method of research you choose is a direct result of the research question you ask, not the other way round.

Different types of data and sources

Sources fall into one of two categories: **primary** and **secondary**. Use both in your dissertation in varying degrees (this is determined by the type of dissertation you are writing, and which department you are writing it for). For example, history students may not have to generate their own data but should consult historical documents. Lawyers may be asked to consult legal documents. Students studying education or engineering have to generate their own (albeit very different) data in order to have something to research (unless they use a bank of data that has been collected and given over to public use).

QUICK TIP

Check with your supervisor that using existing data sets is permitted.

Primary data and sources

Dissertation guidelines often specify that students should *show substantial knowledge and critical understanding of primary sources where relevant*. But what are primary sources and where can you find them? Primary sources will, for most students, account for the vast part of your dissertation, no matter which department you are studying in. It doesn't matter if you are working in the humanities or the chemical and biological sciences, where primary sources are concerned the task is the same: you have to analyse and evaluate critically the sources you have chosen to study, and arrive at a logical, well-structured, coherent argument which helps you to prove or disprove your hypothesis, or answer your research question.

Primary sources can be loosely defined as authentic data; for instance, research reports in sciences and social sciences, contemporary accounts of events such as diaries and speeches in humanities, or novels or paintings in the arts.

Primary sources, if self-generated, can appear in various forms. We will discuss this in more detail in Chapter 4.

Secondary sources

Secondary sources interpret, analyse and draw conclusions from primary sources. They include textbooks, journal articles and book-length arguments.

QUICK TIP

While secondary sources are of fundamental and vital importance to your dissertation, it is important to distinguish between fact and opinion. Make sure that the argument presented in the secondary source is consistent with the evidence, and that there isn't an unnecessary amount of bias.

All students rely on secondary sources for their background reading and for constructing an argument, because in the world of academia you have to cite and quote from previous research. But for those students writing in the humanities, you may have to rely on secondary sources more than students writing in other disciplines. This is because you may end up writing a dissertation which is theoretical and based on secondary sources, with only one primary source at the core. If this is the case, speak to your supervisor about how you should approach this type of dissertation.

Tips for top scores

■ Set your question before designing a research proposal and strategy. Doing it the other way round will mean that your research is out of context.

■ Read studies that are similar to your own to find out which methods they used. Pay attention to any pitfalls that the researcher discovered and don't repeat the same mistakes.

■ Reassess your methods at regular intervals to see if they are providing the information you need to answer the question and initiating new avenues of exploration that are better suited to answering the question.

✓ Dos	✗ Don'ts
✓ Find out what type of research approach your supervisor expects you to use.	✗ Let one method take precedence if you are using a mixed approach.
✓ Analyse your research question and decide if qualitative or quantitative methods will answer it most effectively.	✗ Imply an assumption in your research hypothesis – start from a neutral position.
✓ Watch out for bias in secondary sources.	

PART 2

The research process

Having a great idea to research is only the first step towards writing a dissertation – putting it into practice is the second. Part 2 shows you how to transform your idea into reality by choosing the right research method for your dissertation. It also helps you to put your dissertation in context.

4 Choosing your methodology

This chapter looks in more detail at various methods of data collection and discusses the situations in which they are most applicable.

Before you think about how you can turn your ideas into practice, take a few practical considerations into account, as these could have an impact on the decisions you make.

- The time frame: if you have limited time you should build a research proposal which is not time intensive.
- Your resources: if you have limited resources you should build a research proposal which uses only the resources you have access to.
- Your aim: think about what you are trying to achieve and how you can achieve it. If your aim is small, will you have enough content? If it is large, will it be detailed enough?
- How research is carried out in your discipline: ask your supervisor and read around the subject to see whether there is a particular or accepted method of research you should use.
- How you will analyse the data you collect (if you are collecting data): if you need to use computer software to help you present the numbers, make sure you can afford to buy it (if it isn't free) and are able to use it (if you don't yet have the necessary skills). Take advice from a tutor or supervisor on which programmes are the best.

Your research proposal must meet the needs of your research question or hypothesis, so at this point go back to the aims and objectives you made at the end of Chapter 2 and think about how they can be worked through to enable you to answer your question or test your hypothesis.

Research methods

By familiarising yourself with the advantages and disadvantages of each of the most common methods of data collection, you should be able to design a method that is tailored to the needs of your own individual research aim and question.

For example, an observation can be very useful for a social scientist, especially someone studying psychology. A focus group could be used by an arts or humanities student who wants to know about the impact a certain text had on a group of readers, as opposed to on an individual. Scientists may find interviews helpful, especially if they are dealing with human subjects, and a case study could be useful for a student of medicine as well as for a student of business.

The questionnaire

A questionnaire can be used for both quantitative and qualitative research purposes and is commonly associated with, but not limited to, social science and humanities subjects. It can be a successful way of collecting data from a wide range of participants (as long as your questions are suitably worded).

> **QUICK TIP**
>
> There is no fixed length to a questionnaire, but you should check with your supervisor that you have neither too few nor too many questions.

Question types

Questionnaires can be set up with both open and closed questions, and can generate both numeric and non-numeric data. The type of question you use depends on the type of answer you are looking for. If you are more interested in numbers and figures (quantitative data), use closed questions. If you are more interested in individual responses and depth of attitude (qualitative data) use open questions.

Closed questions:

- force a respondent to select from a choice of answers
- help consolidate thinking towards a given subject
- generate data which is easier to analyse than open questions
- speed up the data collection process by limiting the thinking time a participant needs for each question.

For example: *On a scale of 1 to 5 (1 being unhappy and 5 being very happy), state how happy you are with your current bank.*

Open questions:

- ask respondents to reflect on their emotions
- enable the respondent to be truthful about their feelings
- do not contain any bias (because they are subjective by nature)
- qualify how strongly a respondent feels towards a given topic.

For example: *Can you explain how the feedback from your tutor has helped you to improve your English writing skills*?

Wording a questionnaire

The wording of a questionnaire is not as easy as it looks. When wording your questions, make sure that:

■ the questions are straightforward and neutral – i.e. the phrasing shouldn't deliberately support your pre-assumed conclusion

■ the level of detail required from the respondent is stated clearly

■ definitions are given where needed so what you are asking is clear

■ the questions are relevant to your aim.

Distributing a questionnaire

There are three common ways of administering questionnaires.

1. You can stop people in the street and ask them questions, or ask the questions over the phone (this is different from an interview): these methods are efficient in terms of return rate, but are time consuming. Be aware that being physically present can influence the way in which participants fill in the questionnaire, especially if the information is sensitive.

2. You can put the questionnaires in the post or in a pigeon hole at work or university: in this case the respondent may be more honest in their replies, but this method doesn't guarantee a 100% return rate. (Neither does it guarantee that the questionnaires are filled in correctly!)

3. You can conduct the survey online: this method is user-friendly (they can be filled in when it is convenient to the respondent), but do note that your department may insist on having the results as appendices, which means you need to print a copy of each response.

The interview

Questionnaires are commonly followed up by an interview or focus group (see page 34 for more on these). Interviews are a form of qualitative data collection and give more detail about previously asked questions or interesting points that came out of the questionnaire. They can provide more information about vague findings and are usually conducted one to one, or one to two (more than two interviewees can be difficult to control).

The number of interviews you conduct will depend on what you are trying to achieve with your research. If you are interested in the opinion of one particular person, you only need to interview that person. If not, it is a good idea to interview at least two people (preferably more) to account for any bias.

Identifying the people you want to interview depends on the aim of your research and perhaps also on the results of your questionnaire.

QUICK TIP

Don't go overboard with the number of interviewees – interviewing is a time-consuming process and you may run out of time!

Record any interviews you conduct as you may have to transcribe them later (and you're unlikely to remember everything). Have a trial run beforehand to check the equipment is working correctly and the sound quality is reasonable.

QUICK TIP

Check the rules and regulations in your department regarding the transcription of any interviews. Most institutions insist that interviews are transcribed – this can be time consuming so factor in enough time to do this.

The focus group

Focus groups are a form of qualitative research and are made up of a group of people you have chosen to supply further data for your research. Information collected in focus groups is subjective and opinion based, which can be both a positive and a negative, depending on the nature of the research you are undertaking. A focus group usually meets several times and is helpful if you are undertaking a tracking project or are interested in how opinions change over a period of time.

The number of people you have in your focus group will depend on the aim of your research and is something you should discuss with your supervisor. Remember that too many people will be difficult to control, especially if there is a very outspoken member of the group, so three or four people is probably an ideal number.

Prepare a list of questions and discussion topics ahead of time and don't let the conversation deviate from the topics on your list. If it does, gently guide it back on track. Remember to document everything that is said. One way to do this is to record the discussion, but make sure you get the group's permission first.

The observation

The observation can play an important role in research. By watching an animal, organism or person in their natural environment and observing their behaviour and interaction (either in person or by using a video camera), a researcher can obtain a realistic picture of the subject. On the negative side, observation is a time-consuming and demanding way of collecting data, but on the plus side it can yield exciting and dramatic results. Because of the timescale involved, observation is not always practical for undergraduate research. Observation can influence the way in which the observed subject behaves, which compromises the data collected. So, where possible, try to put yourself or the video camera in a position that is as unobtrusive as possible.

The case study

The case study is an in-depth look at the way in which a particular group of people behaves (for example, a particular class of students or a particular organisation) and assumes that any findings are representative of other groups. Case studies are often used in business studies and in education and can be useful for learning if a particular theory can be applied in a particular environment; for example, analysing whether a teaching method has benefits for a given set of students, or whether a managerial approach has an effect on staff motivation. If you want to use a case study you will have to negotiate an opportunity both to observe this group of people on several different occasions and to gain access to any paperwork you may need to look at. To organise a case study, contact the person in charge of the organisation or group and arrange a meeting to discuss your ideas and aims for the project.

QUICK TIP

Bear in mind that if you are observing a company it may be difficult to get access to paperwork or even to observe the staff, given that information is highly sensitive and staff are very busy. Make sure you ask for permission from the company early in your research process so you can change your plans if need be.

The experiment

Experiments, though seen as the archetype of scientific research, are equally useful in other subjects, such as linguistics.

It is common practice to stage two different experiments: the controlled experiment and the experimental experiment. The experimental group is the group on which you test a variable factor, and the control group undergoes the same experiment without the variable factor (allowing you to observe the effect of the variable factor).

Experiments are generally devised to try to prove or disprove a hypothesis, therefore they generally begin with a null hypothesis – a hypothesis that negates the hypothesis you believe.

Example
Hypothesis: eating an apple a day keeps the doctor away.
Null hypothesis: eating an apple a day does not keep the doctor away.

A hypothesis is assumed to be true when statistical tests are applied and a high probability ($p>0.5$) is found. The type of test you use will depend on your discipline, so consult your handbook or check with your supervisor.

QUICK TIP
It is fine to use more than one method of data collection if you think your research would benefit from it.

Problems encountered when researching

Students frequently encounter problems when researching. Not gaining access to the specific material you need and not managing to collect the necessary data are typical examples. To avoid these problems allow yourself plenty of time for data collection and have a Plan B in place in case you have to redirect your research at the 11th hour. Problems encountered during data collection are discussed in more detail in Chapter 6.

Ethics

Another area that you must consider when conducting research is that of ethics. Ethical criteria usually state that working with children or vulnerable people involves securing consent before any research can be undertaken. Consult your supervisor for details about ethics and your research proposal. They will be able to tell you if this is something you need to think about more carefully. Ethical criteria also state that you should get respondents' written permission before you record them or use their work in your study.

Sampling

Once you have decided upon your preferred method, or methods, of data collection, start thinking about your 'sample': a group of people chosen to be representative of the characteristics of a larger group. Your sample should reflect a broad section of society, or at least the section of society you are interested in. It shouldn't be too big or too small (the size will depend on the aim of your research). Too big can lead to over-generalisation and too small means it doesn't truly represent the section of society you are researching.

There are two main ways of choosing your sample: randomly and non-randomly. The method you choose will be determined by the aim of your research. Work out who the target of your research is before you define your sample. Think about how you might reach these people. For instance, if you are targeting students, you could hand out questionnaires outside the library.

- Random sampling is good for generalisation and is useful if the target population is large, i.e. it is too big for you to survey or interview everyone. In a random sample you select from a large group and everyone has the same chance of being picked.

- Non-random sampling is useful when there are no (known) differences in characteristics within the sample. Use a system (for example every 10th person) to choose the participants.

> **QUICK TIP**
>
> Don't forget that samples are people – they may not do what you expect them to do!

Recording and storing data

There are a few vital points to bear in mind when it comes to recording and storing the data you have collected.

- Remember to write down everything that you collect as soon after the collection as possible.

- Make sure that this is recorded in two different places and is backed up sufficiently.

- Check that you can read your own data and writing, and that if you use abbreviations you know what they mean.

- If there are any gaps in your data, ascertain why and decide if it is necessary to fill them. Do that as quickly as possible to avoid disruption to your flow of ideas and thought processes.

- Remember to chase up any outstanding questionnaires (or make the decision to go on without them).

> **QUICK TIP**
>
> If you are pressed for time, narrow the focus of your analysis. Make sure that you comment on how much data you collected initially and how and why you are changing your focus.

Tips for top scores

■ Know when to stop collecting data. Your supervisor will not be impressed with the volume of data, but by the quality.

■ Have a test run of your data collection before you go ahead and collect it. This way you can weed out any problems.

■ Send respondents reminders about questionnaires that need to be returned – often it isn't that people don't want to help, it's just that they are busy and have forgotten to return their form.

■ Discuss the limitations and strengths of your methods and your sample in your final dissertation. This will gain you academic credit with whoever is reading your work because it illustrates that you are critically evaluating all stages of the dissertation and are not fooled into thinking that your research is flawless.

✓ Dos	✗ Don'ts
✓ Get to know the drawbacks and advantages of each method of data collection.	✗ Design your methods hastily. This is a process that needs to be well thought out.
✓ Test your equipment before you use it.	✗ Expect your sample to behave and do exactly as you want them to. Expect surprises.
✓ Choose your sample carefully and make sure that it reflects a representative group of people.	✗ Expect everything to run smoothly. Factor in time for problems.
✓ Store your data carefully and in several places.	✗ Waste time. Choose your approach and design your research proposal as soon as you can.

5 Informing your research: reading

To get to know your topic inside out and to build a coherent and critical line of argument, read the leading texts in your chosen area of study and explore the main theories and lines of discussion that exist within them (as discussed in 'Background reading' in Chapter 2).

How reading can inform your dissertation

When you first start reading for your dissertation, you may feel overwhelmed by the wealth of material available. Try to remember that it is not possible to read everything – your supervisor is looking as much at the decisions you make about what to leave out as they are at what you choose to include. To make the most of what you read you should try to:

- identify gaps in the literature
- recognise the various and main theories in your field
- see both sides of the discussion
- critically evaluate existing arguments
- find context for your dissertation (see the section on this later in this chapter)
- learn more about the subject itself
- start to develop your own thesis and line of argument
- become familiar with how to conduct research
- interpret and analyse data
- note how to write up what you've found.

Keeping these points in mind can help you be more objective when you are researching and reading the literature – you can read with different intentions each time you pick up a text and be clear and focused about your goal for that reading session.

QUICK TIP

Be selective about your reading, but at the same time remember that if you are too selective you may find it difficult to find useful texts to read.

Where to begin your search for relevant literature

If you find that you are stuck and don't know what to read or where to begin looking for literature, here are some simple steps you can follow.

- Speak to your supervisor. Not only are they an experienced researcher, but they probably know about your topic and the key players in the debate. This will help you to begin your selection.
- Recognise the difference between primary and secondary sources and decide which are most useful for which aspect of your dissertation. For further detail on this, see Chapter 3.
- Make a list of all the sources you want to read before you begin reading them. If you are a visual learner, turn the list into a diagram, showing how the texts and arguments fit together.
- Recognise the differences between theoretical and practical perspectives. Which sources are informing your theory, and which are informing your methods?
- Note what the leading academics say, what they are currently doing and what they have done in the past. Use this information to help you understand the twists and turns the discussion has taken over the years. Understanding the history of an argument will better inform your own argument and help you to understand and analyse your findings.

- Get to know the library. Learn how to use the library catalogue and electronic databases. If you're unsure, sign yourself up for a training session or ask a librarian to show you. If you can't find what you are looking for, investigate interlibrary loans or arrange to go to a different library.
- Use your library's e-resources, for example online catalogues such as JSTOR and ScienceDirect.
- Familiarise yourself with the key words and expressions linked to the topic you are studying. Follow these leads to find new texts and sources.
- Use the reference list of a particularly helpful source to help you search further.
- For secondary sources, use official websites such as:
  - www.bis.gov.uk
  - www.defra.gov.uk
  - www.food.gov.uk

How to identify useful texts

As time is of the essence when writing a dissertation, it is important to identify relevant texts quickly.

Here are a few tips to help you identify a useful journal.

- Scan the title of the paper: does it sound relevant? If not, move on.
- Read the abstract: this will give you a brief summary of the text.
- Read the discussion and conclusion: if the paper still seems to be relevant, go on and read more.

When looking for relevant books, you can do the following.

- Scan the headings within each chapter. Decide if they are useful or not.

As you read, there are ways to quickly get to the information most relevant to you.

- Take notes and paraphrase rather than copying word for word. This saves time in the long run and helps you avoid plagiarism (plagiarism is discussed in more detail in Chapter 9).
- Write down the reference for everything you read, including page numbers. This is important as you may need to re-read some of the material or cite and reference it (see Chapter 9 for more about references).
- Focus on the main arguments and theories present in the texts. Can you see a theme? Do certain authors agree with or contradict each other? Is there a current debate in the topic area?
- Keep reading if you come across a text that explores a contradictory opinion or reflects a gap in the literature. This enables you to develop your arguments and critically evaluate what is said by each author.

QUICK TIP

Stop reading if you think the text isn't useful – you have only limited time and should read only those texts that inform you.

Setting your research in context

Students sometimes approach their research project as if it were unconnected to any previous studies, or as if it were the first piece of text ever to be written on the topic. This has the effect of making the dissertation seem out of context with the wider topic and other related areas.

To avoid making this mistake, think of your project as a whole, and read plenty of material before you plan anything. Don't view reading for your dissertation as something that can be done quickly and easily. It is a long-term task which runs concurrently with method design, data collection, data analysis and drawing conclusions. Make the connection between what you have read and what you are finding out in your own research, and keep your research question at the forefront of your mind.

Conducting a literature review

Using literature (other people's research and arguments) in your dissertation is essential to creating a sound and reasoned piece of research. Your ability to use and incorporate other literature into your own project will be assessed, so it is important to start reading early and to continue reading throughout the duration of your project. Just like reading for your essays, take notes as you read, but don't try to write the review until you have read enough to fully inform your argument.

For many students (especially social scientists and humanities students), reading other people's work culminates in a literature review. While the term 'literature review' implies that you should review everything you have read, this isn't what is required. Instead, use the literature review to:

■ show you have a thorough understanding of the topic
■ establish what the current debates in the field are
■ provide a rationale for your work
■ clarify relevant concepts and theories
■ identify potential areas for research
■ identify knowledge gaps that demand further investigation

- compare previous findings
- critique existing findings and suggest further studies.

If you have to write a literature review, try to be selective and mention only those points that have relevance to your project. You don't have to discuss everything you have read in detail, but comment on why the authors and texts you use inform your findings and your argument.

As the literature review is relevant to all sections, especially those related to context, hypothesis (see Chapter 2), research aim (see Chapter 2), methodology design (see Chapter 4) and findings (see Chapter 6), it is central to the dissertation process. Even if you are not required to write a formal literature review (this is often the case for scientists and engineers), review the literature in an informal manner, as everything you read informs your thinking and your analysis.

The function of the literature review

Depending on which discipline you are studying, you may need to complete (and in some cases hand in) a literature review before you write your actual dissertation (this is common in the humanities). But whichever discipline you are studying, read extensively about your topic before you begin carrying out any research (as outlined in Chapter 2).

> **QUICK TIP**
>
> In the literature review you are not trying to summarise everything you have read about your topic – you are trying to show that what you have read supports the conclusions you make.

Tips for top scores

■ Remember why you're reading: to inform your logic and your argument and to help you connect your research aim and question to your findings and to previous research. Keep this in the forefront of your mind all the time you are reading.

■ Include your own ideas when conducting the literature review and don't just write a running commentary of what everyone else has said.

✓ Dos	✗ Don'ts
✓ Be selective in what you read.	✗ Waste time when searching for literature. Identify the relevant authors as soon as you can.
✓ Read with different purposes in mind.	✗ Rely on one source of information.
✓ Use available resources, such as library staff, to exploit all possible avenues of study.	✗ Go for quantity rather than quality. If what you are reading isn't relevant, don't continue.
✓ Use other people's work to give your own research a context.	✗ Forget to reference the material when you are making notes.
✓ Familiarise yourself with the key purposes of writing a literature review.	✗ Read for one aspect of your dissertation only. Reading should give you information about all aspects of your dissertation.

6 Data and source analysis

Now you have your data you may be asking yourself: 'What do I do next?' The first logical step after data collection is data analysis. Analysing raw data before you present it is important because it means you place the responsibility of interpretation on yourself, not on the reader. By doing so, you limit the possibility of a reader interpreting data in a different way to the one you had intended. You also increase your chances of obtaining a higher mark because you demonstrate a 'high level of analysis' (a feature which appears on most dissertation assessment criteria).

QUICK TIP

It is the responsibility of the researcher to analyse the data, draw logical conclusions and show how these conclusions answer your research question and relate to your wider topic.

Analysis and theoretical dissertations

If you are working on a theoretical dissertation, or a dissertation that does not involve collecting data, you are still required to engage in the data analysis stage. In fact, besides stating why you chose these sources to study in the first place, this is possibly the most important stage of the dissertation. This is essentially what your whole dissertation is about!

Preparing to analyse

The first thing to remember in the data analysis stage is that you need to be clear and focused. Any lack of clarity will reflect badly on the processes you have undertaken during the methodology stage and could potentially undermine all your hard work. Look back at your aim and your research question and decide if the data you have collected is likely to answer the question you set. If it does not, don't panic. It is perfectly acceptable to have encountered problems along the way, which may have prevented you from collecting the data you need. The examiner knows that the dissertation is a learning process. It can go wrong in places, often through no fault of the student researcher.

> **QUICK TIP**
>
> If your data doesn't answer your question, the examiner will be expecting you to discuss the problems you encountered and adjustments you made. They will also expect you to show how you were able to recover from them.

Common problems with data collection

Problems can occur with data collection, as a result of both poor planning and external factors, so it is sometimes useful to assess your data collection halfway through to check that everything is on track. In some cases it can be useful to begin analysis before you have finished collecting all of your data. This way, you can use the findings you have to inform the collection of more data, a technique often favoured in qualitative research.

Here is a list of some of the most common problems.

- Respondents didn't return the questionnaires in time.
- Respondents didn't fill in the questionnaires correctly.

- The subject you were observing failed to do anything worth noting.
- The numerical differences you were hoping to find were too small to analyse or warrant a 'result'.
- Respondents refused to answer the questions you asked them.
- Your experiment gave different results every time you conducted it.
- You threw away some data because you thought it was unimportant, only to realise later that you needed it.
- You forgot to press 'record' on the tape recorder.
- You tried to collect too much data and were overwhelmed by it, or it became too general.
- The questions on the questionnaire were poorly worded and didn't provide the answers you needed.
- You weren't able to gain access to the documents you needed.
- The documents you looked at were not as you expected them to be or were incomplete.
- The interlibrary loan didn't provide the text you needed.

If you have encountered one of the problems listed above, or something similar, ask yourself why, where, when and how? Think how this could have been avoided and work out how great the impact of this problem has been. Decide if you are able to proceed, perhaps with small changes, or if the effects are more wide reaching, meaning that you may have to start again. Discuss all of this with your supervisor. Remember: they are there to help!

Redefining the question

If your data collection has not answered the research question you initially asked, the most logical solution is to redefine the research question. It is fine to modify your original question, but be prepared to explain how and why you did this. Such an explanation would feature in the discussion section or conclusion (see Chapter 7), depending on the structure of your dissertation.

When revising your question make sure that:

- the new question matches your aim
- it is of suitable complexity to satisfy the criteria of the dissertation
- the new focus fits in with your original ideas and thoughts on the subject.

If at this stage you find out that there is a more fundamental problem with your research – for example your methods simply don't generate data that can in any way answer your research question – you have two options. Either go back and redesign a more appropriate method and begin data collection again, or accept that your methods were flawed. Discuss this in either the discussion section or the conclusion. Time will generally dictate which option you choose, but check with your supervisor first before you go ahead and make any drastic changes.

Where to begin

Knowing where to begin when analysing all of your data can sometimes be a little daunting, especially if you have collected a lot, or have used several texts in your analysis. Here are a few tips to help you on your way.

- If you are working with quantitative methods (perhaps writing in maths, engineering, science or economics), try to find a number that stands out from the others. What does this tell you?

- If you are working with qualitative techniques (perhaps writing in sociology, psychology or education), try to find a respondent who disagrees with everyone else. Is there a reason why?
- If you are writing for business, are there certain areas in which the two companies manage situations very differently? What does this suggest?
- If you are writing an arts dissertation, perhaps in English literature, does the author implement different writing styles in different texts? Why?
- Are there no differences in the results of your two different experiments? What does this tell you?

Before you begin drawing conclusions from the raw data, think about the nature of the conclusions you will make, and about the line of argument you are building (for more information about arguments, see Chapter 7). Decide if your conclusions will be based on what you find in the raw data, or if you need to test these findings before you can accept this as reliable data.

Whatever you decide, you will need to make sure that the conclusions you draw are logical and show sound reasoning. Don't jump to a conclusion that cannot be proven – the analysis section(s) is about sound judgement and clear argument.

> **QUICK TIP**
>
> Remember: you are trying to get the reader and the examiner to believe what you are telling them – they will not be easily persuaded to believe something that is completely implausible, or based on an unsubstantiated judgement.

Presenting the data

Think about the order in which you present your data: decide if you are going to have a findings section followed by a discussion section or if you will present them both in one section. Refer to your dissertation guidelines to help you answer this question.

Those writing in the social sciences will have two separate sections, while those writing in the humanities will probably have one section (which may be broken up into smaller chapters). Scientists, mathematicians and engineers will usually have one, although this depends on the discipline and on the department.

To make sure the presentation of your data is as neat and succinct as it can be, answer the following questions before proceeding any further.

> **QUICK TIP**
>
> Familiarise yourself with the rules and regulations that surround the presentation of data in your department – there may be strict guidelines which you are expected to follow.

- Which specific point are you trying to make and what is its significance to the overall argument you are building?
- What is the best way to represent that point?
- Will your audience (the reader) understand what you have found and what you are trying to say?
- If you were the reader, what would you need to know about your research in order to understand it and believe the line of argument?
- How would you be persuaded to accept the results that are being presented?
- What would make you believe that the results were both valid and reliable?

Using graphs, diagrams and text to show your results

Data can be presented in both words and graphs – you will have to decide which best reflects the findings you have made.

Using words or numbers is not as black and white as it may seem. Graphs may need some explaining and words may need illustrating, so make sure you consider the implications carefully.

Graphs and diagrams

Graphs, tables and figures can help order information in a way that is easy to read, but you will need to decide which type of graph is best for which piece of data. If you are using diagrams, use the full range available, from scatter diagrams to bar charts. If you are unsure about which to use or how to use them, look on the internet – a simple Google search should suffice. Organise a session with your supervisor as a final resort. If you have a meeting with your supervisor, take a few pre-prepared diagrams with you.

> **QUICK TIP**
>
> Make sure you use a suitable numbering system for graphs and diagrams (1.1, 1.2, 2.1, 2.2, etc.), and remember to give each diagram or table a title.

Numeric data can often contain a lot of statistical analysis, especially if you are writing in maths, the sciences, computing and engineering. Even if you are not mathematically minded, you can calculate and analyse statistics in a way that conforms with academic and research conventions. This is important if you are writing in subjects which use qualitative methods, but which expect you to present data in a scientific manner, for example linguistics. Don't be put off or afraid of these methods – computer programmes are user-friendly and information regarding which test to use to produce end results is easily accessible on the web. Try the following sites:

- www.data-archive.ac.uk/media/185474/tramsswebsite_archive .pdf (choose analysis software)
- www.socialresearchmethods.net/kb/stat_t.php

- www.biology.ed.ac.uk/research/groups/jdeacon/statistics/tress4a.html
- www.engageinresearch.ac.uk/section_4/step_by_step_statistics.shtml

Text

If you are using text to show your findings, break the text up into small chunks. Give each chunk a subheading, as this will make the information more digestible for the reader. If you are writing in the social sciences, pure sciences, maths or engineering, consider using flow diagrams in places, especially if you are explaining a relationship between two different things – a picture can often be worth a thousand words. If you are writing in the arts and humanities, write longer pieces of text and construct a coherent argument through the use of evidence, claims and conclusions. We will discuss arguments in more detail in Chapter 7.

If you are presenting the outcome of an in-depth questionnaire, include a transcript of the questionnaire in the appendices so that the reader is able to go back and check for themselves that you have extracted the most relevant information and have not misrepresented what was said originally. Don't forget that making a transcript can take hours of your time. Check whether it is acceptable to transcribe only the parts of the interview you present in your findings.

QUICK TIP

Try to minimise the volume of data you include, and reflect the most significant findings in a simple and easy-to-read format. One way of doing this is to write a summary.

Tips for top scores

- If you have any unexpected findings, be open about them. It is better to draw attention to them by critically evaluating how and why they occurred than to try and cover them up.

- Not all of the data you collect will be relevant to your research question, so make sure that you are selective. If it does not appear to be answering the question or developing your line of argument, put it to one side. Don't throw it away until you are absolutely sure that you will not need it any more.

- Emphasise important findings by putting them in bold, or by underlining them.

- When you are analysing your data, keep going back to your research question or hypothesis. Evaluate how the data is answering your question, or helping to prove/ disprove your hypothesis. Move backwards down the research cycle if you have to.

✓ Dos	✗ Don'ts
✓ Demonstrate a high level of analysis by interpreting the data and telling the reader what it means.	✗ Leave out a discussion of the problems you encountered.
✓ Be clear and focused about what you want to achieve in your results section.	✗ Include findings and results that don't fit in with your argument.
✓ Make sure your data is clearly presented and succinct.	✗ Forget to familiarise yourself with the rules about data presentation in your department.

PART 3

Concluding your dissertation

The final stages of a dissertation pull together all the different elements of the project and combine them in one whole text. Part 3 leads you through this process, showing you how to construct a sound argument, make an outline, and draft and redraft your work.

7 Logic, arguments and the conclusion

Whether you are writing a theoretical or research-led dissertation, you need a well-reasoned, incisive, central line of argument to help you prove or disprove your hypothesis, answer your question, or reach your aim. This argument is fundamental to any claims you make and acts as the link between your initial ideas and final conclusion(s).

University dissertation assessment criteria are quite strict about what is expected in terms of argument. Some of the most common skills you will be expected to display in relation to argument are:

- perceptive and independent thought
- critical evaluation of key evidence
- the ability to grasp complex ideas
- the ability to bring these thoughts, ideas and evaluations together in one synthesised argument.

Your line of argument joins the various sections of the project together, making it one complete whole rather than a set of chapters. It should be sustained and interesting, as well as sound, rational, perceptive and compelling. Ultimately, it is the strength and clarity of your logic which determines the final classification of your dissertation. If you include logic which is unsound, highly questionable, or unsupported by evidence, you weaken the strength of your argument and raise questions about your ability to fulfil the criteria.

Constructing your argument

An argument is a series of logical statements, supported by evidence from which we draw or infer rational and sound conclusions. In the written form, arguments enable us to further our existing understanding and gain new knowledge. They help rationalise new discoveries, consolidate existing theories and enable people to alter the way they think.

To ensure that your argument is logical, reasoned and insightful there are certain steps to follow. Here are just a few of them.

- Your argument should be directly connected to your research aim and should attempt to answer your research question, prove or disprove your hypothesis, or argue the reasons why a theory should be accepted or not.
- Make sure that you are able to justify everything you say in your argument and that, if questioned, you are able to provide valid reasons to support your claims (the things that you believe are true but which you may not be able to verify definitively). Such reasons should be supported by primary or secondary evidence.
- Try to pre-empt where people may dispute your logic and your interpretations of data. If you are able to successfully acknowledge and address these contests, you will strengthen your argument, especially if you have evidence to support your claims.

Let's look at an example of an argument against nuclear power.

There are strong reasons against using nuclear power to generate energy.

- *Radioactive waste is toxic and difficult to get rid of. This has implications for the future of our planet.*
- *There have been two major accidents at nuclear plants in the last 25 years.*
- *After each accident, nuclear waste was released causing irreparable damage to humans and animals.*
- *Nuclear waste can be used to make nuclear weapons which have the capacity to destroy life.*
- *Uranium is an exhaustive commodity.*

Yet there are also strong reasons in support of using nuclear power.

- *It will not contribute to global warming.*
- *It is a cost-efficient way of generating a considerable amount of energy.*
- *The technology already exists and money does not have to be spent on research.*

From looking at these premises, it is possible to conclude that nuclear power in its current state is not a viable means of generating all the energy we need, because it isn't completely safe or accident free. This conclusion is supported by evidence: two accidents in 25 years, both of which have caused irreparable damage.

A sound argument that stems from logical claims supported by evidence is necessary to secure belief in the case you are putting forward. The more compelling your evidence, the more convincing your claim. The more convincing your claim, the less anyone can dispute your argument. If a reader is unable to dispute your argument, they are forced to validate and acknowledge your research.

How to make your logic sound

There are two ways of creating sound, rational logic: deductively and inductively. To build either a deductive of inductive argument, you will need to use premises, claims and conclusions. They are the fundamental elements of both types of argument.

Before we discuss this any further, let's define some key terms.

- **Premise:** a principle or statement that you believe to be true and which leads to a claim.
- **Claim:** what you argue is the most convincing and best answer or statement.
- **Conclusion:** the most logical explanation you can draw from the premise and the claim.

Deductive knowledge, sometimes referred to as uncontested knowledge, is often hard to challenge. Inductive knowledge is less obvious and, if wrong, can lead to weakened arguments.

Deductive logic

Deductive logic is created when the conclusion matches the premise of the argument, or when the conclusion cannot be disputed.

Example 1
Premise: my sister is 36 and I am 34.
Conclusion: my sister is older than I am.

Example 2
Premise 1: sisters are female.
Premise 2: brothers are male.
Conclusion: my sister is female.

The logic in deductive arguments is clear, and for this reason students often feel 'safe' when they are working with it – they know that any opponent of their research and claims will find it hard to build up a case against this type of argument.

Unfortunately, much of what you discover in your dissertation may not be deductive, especially if you are working in a new area of research – you may need to infer conclusions. This means you may have to use inductive logic.

Inductive logic

Inductive arguments take logic beyond that which is immediately obvious. They enable you, through informed decisions, to guess, estimate or suggest what the most convincing truth is, even if you are not entirely sure. Inductive logic involves evaluating evidence and deciding if it is strong or weak. It also involves differentiating between fact and opinion.

To ensure that inductive knowledge is sound and well reasoned, take care to make sure that any claims you make are plausible and that they represent the most convincing truth. Remember that what may appear the most convincing truth to you may not be the most convincing to someone else. Support your inductive logic with as much evidence as possible to help persuade the reader.

Example 1
Premise 1: you have to be extremely intelligent to get a first.
Premise 2: only the top 5% of students in the country get a first.
Conclusion: students who get firsts are among the cleverest people in the country.

Example 2
Premise 1: the sky is very black at the moment.
Premise 2: it usually rains shortly after the sky turns black.
Conclusion: it will rain shortly.

Look at example 1 above. The only way you could validate this statement is by finding the cleverest people in the country and applying some form of test. *'What kind of test would I apply?'* and *'How would I locate the "cleverest people in the country"?'* are just two of the questions that spring to mind – there are plenty more you would have to ask to get to the bottom of this issue. There is no easy way to check that this claim is correct. You have to **judge** the evidence, and **conclude** that this is true. In other words, you have to assess the claim based on the evidence you are being presented with and arrive at the most plausible and logical conclusion – the one you believe to be the 'best'.

Inductive logic can be useful for analysing data and findings. Without inferring conclusions and accepting certain claims and statements as true, it is difficult to build up and develop an argument that may be based on 'new' information.

Inductive logic is also useful when discussing methods and methodology.

Fallacies

If you make a mistake of logic in your dissertation, it can seriously impede the validity of what you say, as well as limit the way you develop your ideas. Here are some of the more serious types of logical mistakes:

- collecting evidence which does not address the research question
- having an argument which is not supported by the data
- drawing conclusions from the data which are highly questionable
- having a weak line of argument which can be easily contested.

To avoid these, make sure that your conclusions illustrate sound logic and reasoned thinking, and that they are linked to the central theme of the dissertation.

> **QUICK TIP**
> Remember: the reader must be able to follow your logic at all stages. If there is a jump or a gap in your logic, they will be lost.

Constructing arguments

When constructing logical arguments in your dissertation it is important that you:

- infer conclusions that are logical
- assume the most obvious conclusion, based on your findings
- conclude an incontestable argument from your findings and reading of primary and secondary sources
- use facts, or conclusions taken to be facts, rather than opinions to represent your findings correctly.

Using other people's claims in your argument

In Chapter 5, we discussed how to use existing research to help set your research in context. Use some of the ideas, themes and claims you found in your research to help build your own argument.

Other people's ideas and insights provide credibility and academic rigour both to your central line of argument and to the conclusions you draw about individual findings. In addition, critically evaluating other sources persuades the reader to believe your claims and conclusions, as

QUICK TIP

Always justify your reasons for using other people's claims and conclusions before including them in your own findings.

they know that it isn't just you arguing the point. Finally, if you can show, through your own research and conclusions, that there is a flaw in someone else's argument, you will make your own claims immediately more viable.

The conclusion: drawing your argument together

Building up a line of argument which connects your initial ideas, your reading, your findings and your conclusions is the first step towards consolidating the whole dissertation process. It may seem a little bit back to front, but you will need to go through this process before you can move into the final sections of your dissertation – making an outline and writing up.

The conclusions you have drawn from your data will, as discussed in Chapter 6, be recorded in your results and discussion, or in the body of your dissertation if it is text based. Meanwhile, the whole line of argument will be commented on in your conclusion, as you tie all of the pieces of the dissertation together.

QUICK TIP

Draw conclusions that are obvious and logical. Only draw unobvious conclusions if you have a lot of evidence to support them.

The conclusion should be relevant to your research question or hypothesis, and should demonstrate how you reached your aim and met your objectives (see

Chapter 2]. It is an opportunity for you to show that you have successfully carried out an independent enquiry and have made the 'academic' leap from essay to extended research paper.

Try to make sure that you don't just reiterate what you have said somewhere else, and at the same time make sure you summarise the main points. Show that you have a thorough understanding of your topic and that you are able to evaluate and analyse critically both its limitations and any problems you encountered.

> **QUICK TIP**
>
> When writing your conclusion, put yourself in the shoes of the reader and think about what they need to know to feel that the dissertation has come to a satisfactory close.

Tips for top scores

■ To attain a first class dissertation, show innovation and creative thinking in the construction of your argument – they appear as features in the 'first/distinction' band of dissertation assessment criteria.

■ Make sure that your argument is analytical rather than descriptive. This means including the 'hows?' and 'so whats?'. Provide evidence to substantiate your claims and analyse why something is the way it is. It isn't enough to say that it is what it is – you have to show how and why.

■ Make sure you know the difference between inductive and deductive logic and don't jump to hasty conclusions that can be contested easily.

✓ Dos	✗ Don'ts
✓ Check that your dissertation has a line of argument.	✗ Mistake an opinion for a fact when dealing with inductive logic.
✓ Make sure that your argument is connected to your research aim.	✗ Infer conclusions that are illogical.
✓ Justify everything you say by using other people's work and your own findings.	✗ Assume a conclusion that is not the most obvious, unless you have a lot of evidence to support your decision.
✓ Construct an argument that is rational and logical.	✗ Construct a weak argument that is easy to contest.
✓ Use other people's ideas, theories and evidence to support your own claims.	✗ Misrepresent information to fit your argument.

8 The introduction, the outline and drafting

The final stages of a dissertation require tying the different threads of your research together in one cohesive piece of text. This includes thinking about what you will write in each of the sections or chapters and how you will use this information to tell the story of your research journey. Don't worry though – whatever you decide, it isn't set in stone. 'Drafting' your work will give you the opportunity to change things.

A good place to start planning what you would like to write (and where you would like to write it) is the outline. But, before you begin consolidating your ideas in this way, think about what you are going to tell the reader in your introduction.

Writing your introduction

The introduction, though often accounting for fewer hours in the process of research than data collection or data analysis, has no less importance. It plays a key role in your dissertation and is integral to its success. An introduction has just a few moments to present your research to the reader and interest them enough to read on. For this reason, it should be a well-organised, clear, interesting piece of text, which:

■ outlines the aims and objectives of the dissertation (objectives are specifically important for scientists, engineers and mathematicians)

- gives a clear statement of the problem or question
- states the rationale of the study
- briefly shows the context of the study
- outlines the problem and question to be explored
- gives the central line of argument
- provides an overview of the dissertation (for example, outlining which information will be found in which chapter)
- starts generally and ends specifically.

To make sure the introduction functions well, there are certain things you shouldn't include in it:

- any conclusions you have found or drawn
- the main evidence you have used
- your main findings or results
- an answer to the research question.

QUICK TIP

It is good practice to introduce your central argument in your introduction. Keep it at the forefront of your mind as you continue to write so that you remain focused on the core issues of the dissertation.

Linking your introduction and conclusion

Most students begin writing up their introduction after they have written their conclusion (see Chapter 7). This is because it is easier to arrive at your conclusions (consolidate your arguments and answer your research question) before you present them to a reader. Working in this way does not suit everybody, but for most people seeing the dissertation as a non-chronological piece of text can have many benefits.

QUICK TIP

When you write your introduction, you will be thinking in the past tense because you have already done all of the work; however, the reader is reading in the present tense, so this is how you should write it.

The introduction and the conclusion, even though appearing at opposite ends of the dissertation, are closely related. What you propose in the beginning must be addressed at the end. The reader should feel a sense of connection throughout the dissertation, as though they are reading one long piece of text (rather than lots of short pieces).

Creating an outline

Making an outline can help you organise and consolidate your thoughts and ideas. This is a useful step as it gives you time to think your research through slowly and carefully.

To make an outline, write down your ideas – get them all on paper in a short space of time with no attention to order. Then begin to order them. This will help you to see what ideas you have and how they all fit together – sometimes you don't know exactly what you think until you see the big picture. Your outline won't form part of your final dissertation and should be a short informal piece of text written only for your own benefit.

QUICK TIP

It doesn't matter if you have been writing up sections of your dissertation as you have been going along – it is still helpful to create an outline, as it can help you double-check that you have included all of the relevant points.

Don't forget that, even though you may write up the dissertation in sections or chapters, it will be read as one large piece of work. So, when you make an outline, make sure the information in each paragraph relates to both the research question and to the other paragraphs within the chapter, and that there is continuity between all the chapters in the dissertation. Your central line of argument should be clear, logical and well developed, and should back up any claims or discoveries you make in your analysis. For more information about arguments, see Chapter 7.

What to include in the outline

Essentially, the outline is a way of organising your thinking. With this in mind, here is a check list of things to include.

- State clearly how many chapters you will include (double-check with the handbook and guidelines provided by your department).
- Divide your word count logically between the sections based on the advice you are given. If you are writing a theoretical dissertation, you may need to give more weight to the analysis of sources than to the reasons you chose them. If you are writing a dissertation in the social sciences, sciences, or other similar disciplines, you will need to give equal weight to your methods, data collection and data analysis.
- Include detailed information about each of the points you will make within each paragraph, and which information you will use to support each of these points.
- Include a sentence which shows how the main point of the paragraph relates to the core point of the dissertation.
- Make a note of which citations you will use and from which sources you will draw your ideas.
- Include references and full information about source material.

Deviating from your outline

When you start drafting, don't worry if you deviate from your outline at any point – this is perfectly natural. But stop and think about why you are deviating. Did you miss something important out of your plan, or are you going off on a tangent? If you missed something out, just rethink and rewrite your outline, remembering to focus on your central idea and theme. If you are going off on a tangent, ask yourself whether this tangent is necessary and/or relevant to the central theme, research question or hypothesis.

Drafting

Now that you have planned your dissertation and are clear about how your ideas and research processes fit together, it's time to put pen to paper and begin the drafting process. As we mentioned earlier, nothing is set in stone, at least until your dissertation is sent off for binding! By drafting and redrafting, you can rearrange information as many times as you like, making sure that everything you want to say gets said.

Drafting gives you the time to remove faults or careless errors of judgement, logic or presentation. This minimises the potential for criticism.

The drafting process is very important when writing a dissertation because it allows you to:

- put down your ideas on paper first, without having to worry too much about how well they are connected
- write without worrying too much about repeating words over and over again (they can be changed later)

- write without worrying if what you are writing is too informal (tone is very important – you will need to make the language more 'academic' as you redraft)
- write without worrying about your grammar
- find your voice (as discussed in Chapter 9)
- reorganise your ideas.

There is no limit to the number of times you can redraft your work, but ideally you should have at least three drafts, if not five or six. If you are working to a deadline, time might be a factor. To make sure you have enough time to draft and redraft your work as many times as you need, build drafting into your timetable of tasks (see Chapter 1). However many drafts you make, stay focused on your aim.

QUICK TIP

Try to leave a couple of days between drafts to give yourself a chance to look at your work with fresh eyes. Leaving only a matter of hours between drafts can lead to mistakes as you can't see the wood for the trees!

When drafting, don't be frightened of removing large chunks of text that took you a long time to write – sometimes you have to do this to meet the word count or make your text more cohesive. If you remove parts of your text, make sure that the dissertation still makes sense and that you are still answering the central question or hypothesis. Always keep a copy of the original document (perhaps call it 'draft 1-old') so you can reverse any changes you make.

QUICK TIP

Each time you draft you should focus on a different aspect of the dissertation, for example style, content or cohesion. This will make the process more manageable.

Drafting and your supervisor

If you are lucky enough to have a supervisor who agrees to read drafts of your work, find out well in advance exactly what they are going to read – some supervisors may read a full draft copy of your dissertation, while others may read drafts of various chapters. Once you make an agreement, plan your time carefully and make sure that you allow sufficient time for your first draft – you won't be given a second chance! If your tutor gives you feedback on your drafted work, act on this as soon as you can, otherwise you may forget what they tell you.

Tips for top scores

■ Show your outline to your supervisor and check that you are on the right track before you begin your first draft.

■ When writing your introduction, try not to 'front' your most important findings and evidence: you don't want to reveal all of your secrets at the start.

■ Don't try to get your work perfect in the first draft: this will take up precious time and effectively means you miss out the drafting process, which is valuable in allowing you to reappraise your dissertation as you go.

✓ Dos	✗ Don'ts
✓ Break down the project into manageable chunks – they make it easier to track progress.	✗ Try to write your introduction until you have written your conclusion.
✓ Make several drafts of your dissertation.	✗ Give an answer to the research question in your introduction.
✓ Make sure your introduction addresses the aim of your research.	✗ Leave it too late to hand the drafts in to your supervisor.
✓ Show your central line of argument in the introduction.	✗ Put off getting started – it will only make the task seem harder.
✓ React to feedback you receive from drafts.	✗ Be frightened to remove large chunks of text, even if you worked hard on them.

9 Writing up: finding your voice, referencing and the final edit

The finish line is now in sight! However, it is important as you create the final draft of your dissertation that you keep concentrating and pay attention to detail. You can lose valuable marks through sloppy presentation and poor referencing – falling at the final hurdle can be costly. Here's some advice on how to polish your work so it has the best possible chance of achieving top marks.

The final draft

While the final draft isn't more important than any of the others, there are certain extra things you need to consider as you work through it. They are:

- ensuring that the introduction introduces the main themes (see Chapter 8)
- rewording parts which just don't read that well
- removing any unnecessary repetition
- checking the work against your outline (see Chapter 8), making sure you have included all of the main points you wanted to make
- ensuring your ideas are explained in a simple way which is easy to follow
- making sure your 'voice' is clear throughout (see more on this in the next section)

- making sure paragraphs flow from one to the next
- checking that all chapters are clearly signposted
- ensuring there is continuity across the chapters
- ensuring that the conclusion draws the main themes to a close
- finalising references, making sure they follow convention (see more on referencing later in this chapter)
- checking that all sources cited in the dissertation appear in the reference list
- making sure there are no references in the reference list that don't appear in the dissertation.

> **QUICK TIP**
>
> Give your work to someone else to read. They may be able to spot errors of logic or typos that you missed.

Your 'voice'

An academic text is a communication between two parties: the writer and the reader. This means that when you are writing up your dissertation, you need to have a clear 'voice' which can be 'heard' above all the other voices in your dissertation. Your voice will explain your argument to the reader, stating your position on the topic and showing which conclusions you have drawn and why. It will show the reader the extent to which you believe the various claims you make, and will guide them through the process of thoughts, actions and analyses you undertook during your dissertation journey. Often, you will use the words of others (through citation – see later in this chapter for more on referencing) to help you express your voice.

> **QUICK TIP**
>
> Your ability to express yourself clearly and precisely will affect the final mark you receive – presentation and communication of ideas are part of the dissertation assessment criteria.

Stylistic devices

Your voice can also be expressed and heard through the actual words that you use, so a good command of English is important. When writing up your dissertation make sure that your English is *'lucid'*, *'precise'* and *'correct'*. Here are some stylistic devices you can use to help you achieve these goals.

- Make sure your writing is cohesive and that it 'flows'. Use linking words, such as *'therefore'*, *'furthermore'*, *'accordingly'* and *'besides'* to show how your ideas are connected.
- Be concise and succinct. Long, complex, clausal sentences are not always necessary. It is often more effective to articulate a complex idea in simple terms. However, short sentences can seem choppy and disjointed.
- Use precise language. Refer to a thesaurus and dictionary to help you identify the exact word you are looking for.
- 'Hedge' your language. Use verbs such as *'may'* and *'might'*, adjectives such as *'possible'* and *'probably'*, and adverbs such as *'likely'* – if you are unsure of the claim you are making. But be careful not to make your voice too vague. A sentence like *'it is probable that x causes y . . .'* stops a reader from contesting your claim outright; however, it also stops you from saying precisely what you think.
- Use the full range of punctuation: semi-colons, colons, parentheses. Punctuation is often less intrusive than repeatedly using phrases such as *'such as'* or *'for example'*.
- Don't use subject-specific terminology without giving definitions. The second marker – the person who double marks your dissertation to make sure you are given a fair grade – may be unfamiliar with the subject area.

Style within the disciplines

Each discipline has its own style. Hopefully you have a good idea of the style of writing used in your discipline as you have been writing essays, exams and coursework for the past few years.

Passive voice versus first person pronoun

Some departments ask students to write from the perspective of a third person (i.e. referring to yourself as 'the writer' or 'the author') or through the passive voice. Others ask students to speak in the first person (using the pronoun 'I').

Passive voice: it has been proven that . . .
Active voice: I have proved that . . .

Passive voice: data was collected and analysed using . . .
First person: I collected data and analysed it using . . .

First person: I undertook an experiment to investigate how . . .
Third person: the writer undertook an experiment to investigate how . . .

> **QUICK TIP**
> Double-check the style of writing you need to use in your dissertation as occasionally it is different from the style you used in your essays. Your handbook of guidelines is a good place to look for this information.

Referencing

Referencing and citation are academic norms and something you will have had experience of while writing essays or reports at university. Here's a quick refresher.

- Citation is the act of quoting from other people's work.
- Referencing involves showing where the citation came from.

The extent to which you refer to other people's work can help determine the final mark you receive on your dissertation and there is a clear difference between a third class dissertation which makes 'some attempt to cite sources' and a first class dissertation, which 'provides thorough citation of sources'.

QUICK TIP

Writing a reference list can take a considerable amount of time and students often miscalculate just how much. When including referencing in your schedule of work, make sure you leave plenty of time, at least one whole day if not two.

Why we need references

Using references shows that you have supported your work, and that you have actively researched the background to your topic. In addition to this, referencing primary and secondary sources illustrates your ability to combine ideas from different places and unify them in one text.

Your examiner may choose to follow up your sources to learn more about the subject. Your references will therefore need to be correct and traceable. If you cite from a text, make sure that you cite correctly. Misrepresenting the original idea is an academic no no! Sources that you refer to in the body of the dissertation should be included in your reference list – but don't include those that you used but didn't cite from.

Find out which referencing system your department uses and which conventions govern this system. Learn how the system works by obtaining a handbook or leaflet from your department (if you are unsure, ask your supervisor). In many departments the Harvard referencing system (see below) is the norm, but some subjects have specific systems, for example MLA (Modern Language Association), IEEE (Institute of Electrical and Electronics Engineers) and OSCOLA (Oxford Standard for Citation of Legal Authorities). You should include a list of references (sometimes referred to as a bibliography) at the end of your dissertation, usually before your appendices.

The Harvard system

Harvard conventions rely on a system of surname, forename initial, dates and italics, and sources appear in an alphabetical order. Here are three examples showing how to reference some of the most common sources: a journal article, a book and a website.

Engels, R.C.M.E., Hermans, R. vanBaaren, R.B., Hollenstein, T. & Bot, S.M., 'Alcohol portrayed on television affects actual drinking behaviour' in *Alcohol & Alcoholism*, 44/3 (1999), 244–249.

Jordan, R.R., *Academic Writing Course Study Skills in English* (Harlow, Essex: Longman, 1999).

Markova, E. & Black, R., *East European immigration and community cohesion* [online]. Available at www.northamptonshireobservatory.org.uk [accessed on 10/06/10].

A word on plagiarism

Failure to adequately reference and acknowledge sources is considered plagiarism – a serious academic offence and one that usually means an automatic fail. Plagiarism is an attempt to pass off someone else's work as your own. Even if you 'borrow' only one or two words, this is still plagiarism. Quite often, plagiarism can happen unintentionally through poor attention to detail, but this makes it no less serious. As a dissertation student, it is your responsibility to familiarise yourself with the guidelines and rules connected with plagiarism.

Universities invest in plagiarism-checking software – it will be hard for you to pass off other people's ideas as your own. You have been warned!

> **QUICK TIP**
>
> Even the analysis of data can draw on the work of others – make sure you cite correctly.

Editing

The last thing you should do before you hand in your dissertation is double-check that you have taken into account your department's presentation guidelines. Have a look at your dissertation handbook or ask your department for a list. Here are some of the things you should be checking for.

- Are you over or under your word count? Do you need to remove or fill out any sections?
- Have you noted your word count? Is it in the correct place according to the guidelines?
- Is there a title page? Is the title on it?
- Are all the pages numbered?
- Is your work double line spaced?
- Does it have the correct margins?
- Do you have the correct number of chapters?
- Do all of the chapters begin on a new page?
- Do they all have a title?

- Have you cross-referenced any part of your dissertation? Do the page numbers tally?
- Do you have a reference list?
- Is it in alphabetical order and does it follow the conventions your department uses?
- Are there any appendices? Are they labelled? Does each one start on a new page?
- Do you have the correct number of copies to hand in?

Once you are confident that everything is present and correct, off you go to hand it in! Good luck!

Tips for top scores

- Ask your supervisor how many references they expect to see in your dissertation.

- Keep the reader in mind when writing as they are your audience. Try to think about your dissertation from their perspective – this should help you not to miss out on important information.

- Know when to 'step away' from your dissertation – otherwise, you will be writing forever (or at least right up until the deadline – which is best avoided!).

✓ Dos	✗ Don'ts
✓ Make sure you leave enough time to write up your references.	✗ Use the wrong referencing convention.
✓ Make sure you have a writer's voice and that it is heard.	✗ Forget to check the style of writing you are expected to use.

Dissertation Q & A

How do I choose a topic?

Think about the topics and subjects that interest you, as well as the subjects you are good at. Read around the subject to find a gap in the research, or a niche area which you can make into an independent enquiry.

How do I know which data collection methods to use?

If you want to ask lots of people their opinion about a given topic, you should use a questionnaire. If you want to know about people's feelings, you should conduct an interview or focus group. If you want to learn about how animals behave in their natural habitat, you should observe them.

What do I do if I'm not collecting my own data?

Use primary data collected by someone else, or official documents – perhaps historical documents or acts of parliament. If you are in arts and humanities, you could analyse a film or book and then use critiques of the film or book to guide your study.

What do I do if my data collection goes wrong?

Stop. Assess the situation and think about how 'wrong' your data collection has gone. If your data is only a little off topic, revise your aim so that the data you have collected better reflects it. If it is completely off topic, decide if you have time to start again. If not, bite the bullet and discuss your mistakes in detail in your findings/data analysis section.

What should I do if I don't get on with my supervisor?

Decide if things are as bad as they seem. Could you agree to disagree? If not, get in touch with the course convenor and see if you can get a different supervisor. Or, talk your problems through with a friend.

I'm running out of time: can I get an extension?

You will be given an extension only if there are genuine reasons (extenuating circumstances) for not meeting the deadline. If you are running out of time, refine your research aim and discuss the revisions in your conclusion.

How do I know when I'm finished?

There are certain elements that must be included in the dissertation: the introduction, the body (the analysis) and the conclusion. Depending on which discipline you are writing in, you may also have a methodology section, a findings/results section, and a discussion. Once you have fulfilled these criteria, are happy that you have addressed your question or problem thoroughly, and have reached your aim, then you are finished.

How can I stay on top of my bibliography?

Keep detailed notes of what you read, noting down the author, title and page number. Use reference management software such as EndNote to make this task easier (most universities have this installed on their computers).

Glossary

Abstract
A short summary of the dissertation that outlines the most important parts of the research and that appears at the beginning of the written paper.

Argument
A point of view with supporting premises which is intended to persuade others.

Assessment criteria
The dimensions that are used to judge how well a student has achieved the learning goals of the dissertation.

Bias
An attitude or opinion found in academic texts which shows prejudice towards one thing, person or group.

Claim
A belief that the speaker/writer believes to be true based on premises.

Critical thinking
The need to think analytically and to identify and evaluate evidence to support an argument.

Ethics
A system of rules that determines how you should conduct research when working with people, especially children and vulnerable adults.

External motivation
Motivation to complete a task that is generated by external factors, such as a reward or prize, or sense of having gained something tangible.

Independent enquiry
An autonomous piece of research that is carried out over a period of time and often involves empirical research. Otherwise referred to as a dissertation or research project.

Intrinsic motivation
Motivation to complete a task for no other purpose than to learn more about the task and its subject.

Literature review
The section in some social science dissertations that makes a critical summary of the books and articles that have been read and that helps to support the central line of argument.

Non-numeric data
Data generated by qualitative research which is made up of unquantifiable and unmeasurable data, often generated by results from open questionnaire questions, interviews, focus groups or case studies.

Numeric data
Data generated by quantitative research which is made up of quantifiable and measurable data in the form of numbers and figures, often generated by closed questionnaire questions and experiments.

Primary data/sources
Authentic data, such as research reports, contemporary accounts of events such as diaries and speeches, and books or paintings.

Premise
A statement used in an argument that you believe to be true and that leads to a claim.

Qualitative research
The type of research commonly found in (but not limited to) the arts, humanities and social sciences, which categorises unmeasurable data and makes observations about broader social phenomena, such as identity, political ideologies or religion.

Quantitative research
The type of research commonly used by (but not limited to) scientists, engineers and students of medicine, which categorises measurable data generated through carefully planned and executed experiments.

Raw data
Data that has been collected for the purposes of research but hasn't yet been subjected to analysis or refining.

Research proposal
A document written by a researcher which outlines in sufficient detail the rationale, research aim and research question of a piece of research and which also gives details about the methods to be used.

Sample
A finite part of an entity, group or item which is studied to give an accurate reflection of how the larger group, entity or item behaves.

Secondary data/sources
Secondary sources interpret, analyse and draw conclusions from primary sources. They include textbooks, journal articles and book-length arguments.

LEARN ALL THE ESSENTIALS

LEARN ALL THE ESSENTIALS

STUDENT ESSENTIALS

Get to grips with core skills for study success

IN 1 HOUR

STUDY SKILLS

Matt Potter

Including how to:

Prepare for lectures

Develop presentation skills

Improve time management